INCENDIARY

Adam Szymkowicz

BROADWAY PLAY PUBLISHING INC
224 E 62nd St, NY, NY 10065
www.broadwayplaypub.com
info@broadwayplaypub.com

Cover photo by Mitchell Harvick

First edition: July 2017
I S B N: 978-0-88145-726-1

Book design: Marie Donovan
Page make-up: Adobe InDesign
Typeface: Palatino

A workshop production of INCENDIARY at The Juilliard School opened 14 February 2007. The cast and creative contributors were:

ELISE .... Jessica Love
JAKE .... Adam Driver
CARRIE... Sena Rich
GARY... Alejandro Rodriguez
JANE/SALLY/LIZ..Anastasia Scott
JIMMY SPLINTERS/TOM/BRIAN/PAUL............Sean Parker
TOMMY TEN TOES/STU/TED/NEAL .... Geoffrey Murphy

Director.. Kip Fagan
Stage managers ....April Kline & Wendy Ouellette

Southern Rep (Artistic Director, Aimée Hayes; Managing Director, Marieke Gaboury) in New Orleans produced a radio play version of INCENDIARY which opened 19 November 2010. The cast and creative contributors were:

JAKE	Michael Cerveris
ELISE	Aimée Hayes
GARY	Chad Schiro
CARRIE	Jessica Podewell
JANE/SALLY/LIZ	Lara Grice
TOM/BRIAN/PAUL	Todd D'Amour
STU/TED/NEAL	James Bartelle
Stage directions	John Neisler
Director	Damon Arrington
Sound design	Mike Harkins
Lighting design	Joan Long
Stage manager	Jamie Montelpre
Production design & Sound foley	Sarah Zoghbi

INCENDIARY was subsequently produced by
Wishbone Theater Collective at Stage Left in Chicago.
It opened 18 May 2012. The cast and creative
contributors were:

ELISE ....Laurie Jones
JAKE .... Paul Vonasek
CARRIE.. Sara Kaplan
GARY.. Brandon Little
LIZ..Erin Lovelace
TOMMY TEN TOES/PAUL............................Aaron Weiner
JIMMY SPLINTERS/NEAL ....Pete Geovagnoli
TED/STU..John Mark Sawyer
BRIAN/TOM ....Joe Dusek
JANE/SALLY ....Jazzma Pryor

Director...Katie Jones
Assistant director.. Mitch Harvick
Dramaturg...Margaret McCall
Stage manager... Tim McCalister
Set design ....Tim Lane
Lighting design/Props...............................Holly McCauley
Costume design..Mandy Stertz
Sound design.. Theresa Ebenhoeh
Fight choreographer .... Brian Barber
Technical director/House manager ....Rush Marler

CHARACTERS & SETTING

ELISE
JAKE
CARRIE
GARY
TOM/BRIAN/PAUL/JIMMY SPLINTERS
STU/TED/TOMMY TEN TOES/NEAL
JANE/SALLY/LIZ

All characters are in their 30s or 40s but can be played by much younger actors. Actors can be any race. I suggest the cast be as diverse as possible.

New York City. A therapist's office, a police station, a fire station, the street, JAKE's apartment, CARRIE and GARY's apartment, a bar.

These can be suggested minimally.

Time: The present

A Note about the fire: Probably, the stage really can't be set on fire, unless you have a fantastic budget and a very talented fire-tamer. The closest possible substitution should be found with flickering orange lights and sound, maybe some smoke, perhaps those orange strips of paper moved by a fan. Or nothing and let the audience imagine it with the help of a light and/or sound cue.

Special thanks in no particular order to—

Everyone involved in the readings, productions and presentations at Juilliard, Ars Nova, South Coast Rep, Studio 42, LABryinth Theatre Company, Southern Rep, Wishbone Collective, Available Light Theatre. Richard Feldman, Chris Durang, Marsha Norman, Joe Kraemer, Kip Fagan, my class at Juilliard, The Ars Nova Play group, Kim Rosenstock, Kristen Palmer, Seth Glewen and everyone at Gersh, Marieke Gaboury, Tish Dace, John and Rhoda Szymkowicz, Kathy Hood, James Gregg, Jerry Shafnisky, Julianne Just, Becky Guy, Damon Arrington, Felix Solis, Beth Cole, Joselin Reyes, Sidney Williams, Michael Puzzo, Kelley O'Donnell, Carlo Alban, Julian Acosta, Rebecca Marzalek-Kelly, Chris Tsokalas, Joy Suprano, Stephen Bel Davies, Nilanjana Bose, Nick Choksi, Stephen King, Dion Mucciacito, Han Tang, Susan Louise O'Connor, Todd D'Amour, Travis York, Kelly Rae O'Donnell, August Schulenburg, Flux Theatre Ensemble, Shelley Butler Hyler, Portia Krieger, Moritz von Stuelpnagel, Stephen Willems, Mark Schultz, MCC Theater, Megan Monaghan, Evan Cabnet, Frank Basloe, Stephen Gaydos, Stacey Luftig, Devan Sipher, Aimée Hayes, Paula Vogel, Gary Winter, Joshua Fardon. This play has been kicking around for a while so I'm probably forgetting someone important. So thank you person I forgot who I definitely shouldn't have forgotten.

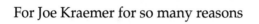
For Joe Kraemer for so many reasons

PROLOGUE

(The lights rise on GARY *in the street looking suspicious, carrying a suitcase across the stage.* LIZ *approaches from the opposite direction also carrying a suitcase. When they get to the center, they put their suitcases down and pick up each others' cases and keep walking like nothing happened.)*

1

(A therapist's office. CARRIE *is in professional attire.* ELISE *wears a fireman's hat, a long raincoat and big rubber boots.)*

CARRIE: Before we start, congratulations on the promotion, Elise.

ELISE: Thank you. It was in the—

CARRIE: Yes, I read it. The youngest fire chief in New York City ever. Very impressive.

ELISE: Thank you.

CARRIE: You must be very proud.

ELISE: Things have been going well.

CARRIE: That's always good to hear. What else is going on? You missed last week's session.

ELISE: Been a lot of fires recently.

CARRIE: I see. And…uh these are—

ELISE: Oh, we've been keeping ahead of them. Don't worry.

CARRIE: I'm not worried, I'm asking ab—

ELISE: Although the dating has slowed down, you know since the promotion. Men are threatened by a woman in power.

CARRIE: Let's talk about why you feel that way.

ELISE: I don't think we need to talk about it. I mean it's true, right?

CARRIE: Well, I consider myself a successful woman and I—

ELISE: Jesus Christ. Can we get through one session without talking about your husband?

CARRIE: I wasn't—I'm sorry.

ELISE: I swear.

CARRIE: I'm sorry.

ELISE: Are you really?

CARRIE: I don't think it's relevant to—

ELISE: Am I paying you to ignore and disrespect me?

CARRIE: I'm not— How is your impulse control these days?

ELISE: Oh, come on—

CARRIE: I think it's important to discuss.

ELISE: Have I been starting fires, you mean.

CARRIE: Well, yes.

ELISE: I want to stop. I really do. I'm trying. I really am. But I don't think you understand. A fire is the most beautiful thing ever created. I dare you to show me a work of art that can rival a five alarm fire. You couldn't do it. You just couldn't. And I like art as much as the next person but I wonder always when I see a

Van Gogh or a Rembrant--I imagine, as I'm sure you do, what it would look like on fire. That second before the painting caves in, that would be... it would be... incomparable. But sadly, I don't think any of us will live to see it. We could burn prints, I suppose, cheap gift store prints, but it would just be paper. No melting paint, no disintegrating wood. It's a waste.

CARRIE: Well, I don't know about that.

ELISE: There is nothing in this world like fire. At first it's just a match, an idea, a spark, a little yellow flame, and it need nurturing to grow to an inferno. Those oranges, those yellows, those cores of blue don't just happen by themselves. They take planning. They take skill. They take love. I am not some Zippo-flicking fourteen year old—no. I am an artist. I can light a fire so precise all that's left of the building is dust while the rest of the block is miraculously untouched. And of course, me and the boys are always around to come and put it out in case anything should happen.

CARRIE: You need to stop.

ELISE: I know. I'm trying. I've been trying. That's why I'm here. You're supposed to help me.

CARRIE: I'm trying to help you. *(Pause)* I'm going to have to go to the authorities.

ELISE: You don't have to do that. I'll stop, I swear.

CARRIE: I have to. It's been over a month. I should have gone the first day you came in here.

ELISE: It was my last. I won't do another one. Please.

CARRIE: You promise?

ELISE: I swear. You should have seen it though. It's so beautiful. So beautiful.

2

(The Police Station. JAKE sits at his desk, his head in his hands. He takes a swig from a whiskey bottle and then puts his head back in his hands. TOM, JANE and STU enter dressed as police.)

TOM: Detective.

JAKE: Tom.

JANE: Detective.

JAKE: Jane.

STU: Detective.

JAKE: Stu.

TOM: Hittin' the bottle pretty hard.

STU: Drinkin' like a fish.

JANE: Sumptin' on your mind?

JAKE: No, no. Yes. It's this damn arsonist.

STU: Oh, I thought you were thinking about your ex-girlfriend again.

JANE: Stu!

STU: What?

JANE: Really.

STU: No, I'm glad you're thinking about the arsonist. I'm glad he's thinking about the arsonist.

JAKE: Not that it's doing any good. Bastard is burning down my city building by building and burning all the evidence in each masterfully designed fire.

TOM: Yeah, he's making you look pretty bad.

STU: Cripes, I wouldn't want to be you.

JANE: No leads, huh?

JAKE: None. Real professional jobs, all of them. And done with such precision.

TOM: And malice.

STU: Bloody anarchy.

JANE: Hope he fries, the flaming bastard.

TOM: Ain't no reason for a man like that to live even.

STU: Sick is what it is.

JAKE: I dunno. You know what really gets me?

JANE: What?

TOM: What?

STU: What?

JAKE: The unmitigated gall. Coming to my neighborhood starting fires. We work hard to keep order.

JANE, TOM, STU: We do.

JAKE: The size of the balls on this bastard comes to my district lighting fires. Causing chaos. The streets full of screeching fire engines. The danger of speeding traffic. The heat of the fire itself. Little old ladies crossing the street. Fire hoses. Dalmatians. Ladders. The whole thing leaves a bad taste in my mouth. What kind of person causes such chaos? It's sick is what it is. And not a clue to be found anywhere. It's days like this I rethink my career choice. Maybe I could design rare vases or be a scuba instructor. I'd give it all up tomorrow but then the arsonist would just get away.

JANE: You'll get em, Jake.

STU: Don't worry.

TOM: Hang in there, slugger.

(The phone rings.)

JAKE: Hello. I'll be right there. *(hangs up the phone.)* If you'll excuse me, I got a fire downtown I got to get to.

3

(CARRIE and GARY sit across from one another at their dining room table. There are plates of food in front of them)

CARRIE: Gary, you're not threatened by me because I'm a strong independent woman, are you?

GARY: Shut up and get me my dinner.

CARRIE: It's in front of you.

GARY: Oh. So it is. What is it?

CARRIE: Meat.

GARY: What kind of meat?

CARRIE: Gary, we've been together for five years now…

GARY: It's kind of gray.

CARRIE: And I was wondering…

GARY: And yellow.

CARRIE: What do you do all day long?

GARY: I told you never to ask me about my work.

CARRIE: I know, but I just wonder. We have a lot of nice things. And I'm not sure where the money comes from.

GARY: Didn't I say never ask me about my work? I said don't ask me about my work. I said—what did I say?

CARRIE: You said don't ask me about my work.

GARY: That's right. So what are you doing?

CARRIE: Asking you about your work.

GARY: But I told you never to ask me about my work. Don't you remember that?

CARRIE: I do.

GARY: So…

CARRIE: It's just that I was talking to one of my patients today—

GARY: Goddamit, can we get through one meal without talking about your patients?

CARRIE: I'm sorry.

GARY: Seriously.

CARRIE: Sorry.

GARY: Are you?

CARRIE: It's just that I was talking about you and I wanted to talk about your work and I couldn't because I don't know what it is.

GARY: I thought we discussed this.

CARRIE: We did.

GARY: I thought we decided.

CARRIE: I'm not so good at deciding. I'm more of a listener.

GARY: We talked about you not asking me about my work.

CARRIE: *(Ashamed)* I know.

GARY: Didn't we?

CARRIE: Yes.

GARY: So…

CARRIE: I'm sorry.

GARY: You know what? Just this once, okay? Just this one time you can ask me about my work. Only this once, okay? This one time. What did I say?

CARRIE: I can ask you about your work.

GARY: This one time.

CARRIE: Right.

GARY: Say it.

CARRIE: I can ask you about your work this one time.

GARY: Right.

CARRIE: Okay. What's your work?

GARY: I'm an executive at a corporation.

CARRIE: Oh, you are?

GARY: Yes.

CARRIE: Huh! Well what do you know? That sounds kind of boring actually.

GARY: Well… it's…

CARRIE: Deadly boring.

GARY: No, it's… um—

CARRIE: So what exactly do you do all day long?

GARY: I'm afraid I can't tell you that.

CARRIE: But—

GARY: It's classified.

CARRIE: Oh. It is!? Does that mean—

GARY: *(Starts to eat.)* Goddamit! Now this meat is cold.

CARRIE: I'll warm it up.

4

(In the dark, the sound of a firetruck rushing to a fire, sirens screaming. ELISE, BRIAN, TED, and SALLY enter, pull out hoses, set up ladders. Enter JAKE.)

ELISE: *(To JAKE)* Get out of the way.

JAKE: Who's in charge here?

ELISE: I am. Now get the fuck out of the way.

(JAKE steps back.)

ELISE: *(Into radio)* We got a five story brick building with flames visible on the first and fourth floor, corners A and C. It is breathtakingly beautiful but it could be the death of us all today if we're not careful. *(To firefighters.)* Hose!

TED: Hose!

ELISE: Up in front! Ladder!

BRIAN: Ladder!

ELISE: I need two front, two top.

SALLY: Two front, two top.

ELISE: You, take Akim and Julio and hit the building from the A corner. Soon-Yi, get that hose in there. Suffocate her. Strangle the life out of her! There now. To the right more.

JAKE: Wow. I've never been this close.

ELISE: Step back. Team three, move in!

JAKE: Kind of takes your breath away, don't it? Kind of makes you rethink what you know about the world and your place in it. Just so powerful! What's the word? What's the word I'm looking for?

ELISE: Fiery?

JAKE: Just this huge force of nature. I felt that way at the Grand Canyon too and the Smithsonian and at Niagara Falls. You ever been? The Petrified Forest is nice too. You should go sometime, you know, when you're not so busy. Maybe I could take you. I'm sorry. I didn't mean to say that.

ELISE: Who are you?

JAKE: Jake.

ELISE: Jake?

JAKE: Detective Stratford.

ELISE: You sightseeing?

JAKE: It's my case.

ELISE: I see. You're losing your stream. God dammit. I have to do everything myself. Jorge, you want to keep that going?

JAKE: Chaotic, isn't it?

ELISE: No, that's not chaos you see. No sir. Hey! Where's my backup!

JAKE: So orange. What makes that so hot?

ELISE: That's just the way fire is.

SALLY: It doesn't look like anyone's inside.

ELISE: Thank you Sally.

JAKE: You seem to have it pretty much under control now.

ELISE: Looks that way, don't it? You can never tell though with a fire.

JAKE: Oh, well. Maybe I'll come back when you're more available…to talk.

ELISE: You can stick around. Long as you don't get in the way. There's plenty of fire for everyone.

JAKE: I'm not going to bother you while you're working, but maybe later I could come by and talk to you more about this fire and some other fires and things. I'll come by the fire station and see you.

ELISE: You do that. You come by the station.

5

(The fire station. SALLY, TED and BRIAN are playing cards at a table in the corner. ELISE and JAKE talk nearby.)

SALLY: I see.

TED: I raise.

BRIAN: I call.

ELISE: And there's no leads at all?

JAKE: None.

ELISE: Interesting.

SALLY: I'll take two.

TED: Three

BRIAN: Two.

JAKE: You haven't seen anything suspicious have you? Anyone hanging around?

ELISE: I haven't seen anything.

JAKE: Someone had to have seen something.

ELISE: And there's no hard evidence?

JAKE: It's all been burned up.

SALLY: Five.

TED: I see.

BRIAN: I raise.

JAKE: You know people are talking about you?

ELISE: They are?

JAKE: Always the first to the fire.

ELISE: And the last to leave.

JAKE: They say you're psychic.

ELISE: I do have a knowledge I can't quite account for. It seems like as soon as a fire starts in this city I know about it. I sense it. I feel it. I smell it. Where there's smoke…

JAKE: There's fire.

ELISE: Sure, copper. You got it exactly right.

TED: I fold.

BRIAN: I raise.

SALLY: I see.

JAKE: I like the way you handled yourself earlier today. With that fire.

ELISE: Didn't do it for you.

JAKE: I know. That's part of the draw.

ELISE: Zat right?

JAKE: It's just who you are, isn't it? You were doing what you were doing and it didn't matter if I was there to watch.

ELISE: Why should it?

JAKE: It shouldn't. I admire that kind of concentration to a task. That kind of single-minded focus.

ELISE: I'm guessing you have a bit of that in you as well.

JAKE: That's a good guess.

BRIAN: I see.

SALLY: I call.

JAKE: Would you like to get a drink later?

ELISE: You asking me on a date?

JAKE: Would that be a problem?

ELISE: I just like to be clear about what I'm getting myself into.

SALLY: Full house!

BRIAN: Shit!

JAKE: So what do you say? One drink. Will you meet me?

ELISE: I'll meet you. Bring all the charm you can muster, K?

JAKE: I always do.

6

(At a bar. JAKE *wears a different tie.* ELISE *wears a skirt under her raincoat. She still wears her big rubber boots.)*

JAKE: I had to shoot him. I didn't want to. I still have nightmares about it. But I had to do it. If I had to do it again, I'd do the same thing. It was me or him you see and I decided in that split second it should be him. After all, he was a criminal. I take the law very seriously.

ELISE: Is that right?

JAKE: I'm sure you take your job very seriously too. Being the youngest ever fire chief and all.

ELISE: You read up on me.

JAKE: I am a detective.

ELISE: I found out a little about you too.

JAKE: What's that?

ELISE: You live alone. No pets even. You drink too much. You swear too much. You call your mother on Sundays. You never call your father. Your socks often don't match. You never learned to swim. You've never been married but you had an ex-girlfriend you loved more than anything. She died when a tour boat accidentally caught fire in the Caribbean. You were supposed to be on that boat but you couldn't get the time off. Some nights you wished you had died with her—suffocated and then burned to death. Other times you imagine you could have saved her even though you never learned to swim. You couldn't cope for a while after her death. They gave you time off after you crashed up a coupe or two. Then you spent a little time in a white room with cushy walls. When you returned they gave you fire duty. You have an almost religious need to catch this arsonist. And while I believe you have interest in me, I can't help but think deep down, perhaps subconsciously, you want to be close to me in case it helps your case in the long run. That and I'm the best looking firefighter in New York. Although they didn't print that.

JAKE: Well...I guess you did your homework. Anything else?

ELISE: Yeah. You're an excellent detective. You almost always get your man.

JAKE: I wish that was true. But let's not talk about my work. Why don't you tell me what makes you tick?

ELISE: That's kind of a broad line of questioning. You're going to have to be more probing than that, detective.

JAKE: Probing?

ELISE: I promise I'll stay still.

JAKE: Will you?

ELISE: For the moment. The night is still young.

7

(LIZ *sitting at a table in a café. There is something fishy about her. Enter* GARY. *He stands by her table.*)

GARY: Excuse me.

LIZ: Are you the waiter?

GARY: No. I am a friend of yours.

LIZ: I am only friends with people from Villanova or Austria.

GARY: I am from both places. I was in the orchestra.

LIZ: Please sit.

GARY: (*Sitting, then in a low voice*) Can I speak frankly?

LIZ: (*Also in a low voice*) No. It's not secure.

GARY: Let me just say that some things have been accomplished.

LIZ: Which things?

GARY: The things.

LIZ: All the things?

(Enter PAUL *the waiter.)*

PAUL: Hi. My name is Paul. I will be your server today. What can I get you?

LIZ: Paul, we need a few minutes.

PAUL: Can I get you drinks while you decide?

LIZ: No, Paul. Please come back later.

PAUL: Sure. The special of the day is a pan seared salmon—

LIZ: Please go away. Seriously. I'm serious. Really.

PAUL: Fine.

GARY: Thanks, Paul.

PAUL: Yeah, yeah…

(Exit PAUL.*)*

LIZ: You were saying.

GARY: I was saying. I need another week. But I'll drop off part one tonight.

LIZ: All you have is half of it?

GARY: Yeah.

LIZ: I don't even think there's time to order another drop.

GARY: I'll get it to you.

LIZ: If you can't deliver on time…

GARY: I just need another week.

LIZ: You already had another week.

GARY: One more.

LIZ: How many more times will you say that?

GARY: This is the last, I swear.

LIZ: That's what you said last time.

GARY: It's much harder than you imagine. I've been on a business trip.

LIZ: Listen, are you sure you want to do this?

GARY: Absolutely.

LIZ: Because you're not very good at it. Maybe we should just forget about the whole thing and go our separate ways. You give us the money back and we'll both forget about ever meeting one another.

GARY: No, I can do this.

LIZ: You sure?

GARY: Positive.

LIZ: I'll try to set up another drop. This can't keep happening though.

GARY: I understand.

LIZ: Do you?

GARY: Yes. Are we done here?

LIZ: Get out of here. *(Louder)* You played the trombone in the marching band.

GARY: Yes, and you twirled the flaming baton.

LIZ: Good to see you old friend.

GARY: Likewise. *(He starts to get up.)*

(CARRIE enters, sees her husband GARY dining with another woman as PAUL comes by the table.)

CARRIE: Gary!

GARY: Carrie!

PAUL: Are you ready to order now?

GARY: It's not what it seems like.

CARRIE: It sure seems that way.

LIZ: What is this?

PAUL: Should I get one more place setting?

CARRIE: No, thank you.

GARY: Don't make a scene.

CARRIE: I'm going to make a scene. (*She screams at the top of her lungs. It is blood curdling*)

LIZ: Will you shut her up?

GARY: I can explain everything.

CARRIE: Don't bother. (*She screams again*)

GARY: That's enough. Let's go outside.

CARRIE: I'm leaving! Don't bother coming home tonight.

GARY: But… Carrie!

(*Exit* CARRIE.)

LIZ: This is so unprofessional.

PAUL: Can I get you drinks?

8

(*Back at the bar,* JAKE *and* ELISE *are getting drunk.* TOM, STU *and* JANE *are doing shots.*)

STU: I was never what you would call lucky in love.

JANE: I've been divorced more times than the circus has come to this town.

TOM: I had sex with a clown once.

(*They all do shots in unison.*)

JAKE: I like when you look at me like that.

ELISE: Like what?

JAKE: Your eyes. There's fire in them

ELISE: Most people don't notice that. I blend into crowds. My whole life I've been invisible. The invisible girl and now the invisible woman. The invisible fire chief. I never make an impression. It's just not my personality.

JAKE: You made an impression on me.

ELISE: So it seems. You sure you're not mistaken?

JAKE: You're beautiful

ELISE: Thank you. You're not so hard to look at yourself. It's disarming.

JAKE: It's supposed to be. Sometimes you disarm someone with a karate chop to the wrist and sometimes it's with your good looks and charm. They are just different weapons I have honed.

ELISE: There is no violence in your eyes. There is kindness.

JAKE: I wish you hadn't seen that yet.

ELISE: You don't want me to know you're kind?

JAKE: I don't want you to think I'm weak.

ELISE: On you, it's not a weakness.

JAKE: It's not?

ELISE: I've never met a man like you.

JAKE: I've never met a woman like you either. That's good, right?

ELISE: It could be.

JAKE: But is it? How is this date going?

ELISE: You don't know?

JAKE: I have a hard time reading dames. I understand shapes of steel and progression of fire. I've honed a sixth sense about the presence of brass knuckles and lead pipes. I understand the depth and breadth of hard liquor and loss and can hear the music underneath the hesitant patter of a suspect. But, try as I might, I cannot understand women.

ELISE: I like you Jake, perhaps more than I should allow myself to.

JAKE: You do?

ELISE: I'll be right back. *(Exit)*

TOM: I like big butts. You know, really big butts? Like your wife's butt, Stu.

STU: When no one's home I like to smoke reefer and masturbate to internet photos of exotic-looking women.

JANE: I like to date the kind of man who if it ever came down to it, I know I could kick his ass.

(They down shots.)

(ELISE returns. She hands JAKE her underwear.)

JAKE: What's this?

ELISE: It's my underwear.

JAKE: What do I do with it?

ELISE: It's supposed to be sexy. You're supposed to like it.

JAKE: Oh, I do.

ELISE: Never mind.

JAKE: It's sexy.

ELISE: Just give it back to me.

JAKE: No, I get it. It's sexy. I'll hold onto them if that's okay.

ELISE: Okay.

JAKE: But I could give them back later, if you want them back, after the moment has passed.

ELISE: That's thoughtful.

JAKE: Thanks.

ELISE: Maybe you should kiss me now.

(ELISE *and* JAKE *kiss.*)

JANE: Whoa.

STU: Hey!

TOM: Ho.

JANE: I've never been kissed like that.

(*They do shots.*)

9

(ELISE *and* JAKE *continue to kiss as they move into the space that is* JAKE's *apartment. They undress as they kiss, but* ELISE's *big rubber boots stay on. Then they are making love on the bed, perhaps under the covers, perhaps not. There are groans of pleasure.*)

ELISE: There are many ways to make a fire. Oooh. Friction is good. Ahhh. Although not the most popular. Pressure. We like pressure. Mmmm. You can have an electric fire, sure or gas, grease, a chimney fire. Uuunh. But I like the kind made with intense amounts of friction. Or one solitary strike. Mmmm. Of a match. But yes, the intense pressure of bodies uuummmm colliding oohhh to make a spark uuuuhhh that may or may nnnnmm not set the whole thing whaaaa into a blazing mm pulsing mm creature ah with a mmmm… life of its own.

(*They come.* JAKE *falls asleep. Exit* ELISE)

10

(CARRIE *in her apartment. A knock at the door.* GARY *stands in the hall waiting to be let in.*)

CARRIE: Who is it?

GARY: It's me.

CARRIE: Who?

GARY: Your husband, Gary.

CARRIE: I have no husband.

GARY: Um…yeah you do.

CARRIE: Go away.

GARY: At least let me explain.

CARRIE: There's nothing to say. You found someone younger, someone more beautiful. Good luck with that. I'm very happy for you.

GARY: That's not…Jesus, will you let me in?

CARRIE: No.

GARY: It's about my work. I don't want to talk about it in the hallway.

CARRIE: Your work? (*She opens the door.*)

GARY: Thank you.

CARRIE: You work with her? At your corporation?

GARY: Not exactly. See the truth is… (*Whispers*) I'm a spy.

CARRIE: What?

GARY: I'm a corporate spy.

CARRIE: Oh. That's ridiculous.

GARY: See the thing is I work for this corporation as an executive. Let's call them "the corporation". But really I work for another competing corporation. Let's call them "the other corporation". So by day I work at the corporation but the whole time I'm looking for opportunities to take photos of strategic plans and rows of numbers. Really it's kind of boring but then I smuggle these out to the other corporation and they give me lots of money.

CARRIE: Oh.

GARY: What?

CARRIE: I thought you did something less corporate or more dangerous. Like working for the C I A or maybe the mob.

GARY: I have a very small camera. You want to see?

CARRIE: Maybe later.

GARY: If the corporation found out they would have me killed.

CARRIE: Oh, well that's something anyway. *(Pause)* They would really have you killed?

GARY: No doubt about it.

CARRIE: Let's go to bed. It's late.

GARY: Okay. Good. Get in that bedroom, woman.

CARRIE: Just sleeping. No funny business.

GARY: But I'm a spy.

CARRIE: I know you are, baby. But not the dangerous kind.

GARY: Maybe tomorrow?

CARRIE: We'll see. You really think they would try to kill you?

(CARRIE *follows* GARY *into the bedroom.*)

11

(ELISE *is lighting a fire.*)

ELISE: Burn, burn, burn. I will raise you from a flame and nurture you. Feed you until you grow up into a real fire. And then you will burn, burn, burn. You will scratch the sky and you will scathe the ground and you will be warm and good and you will make me very happy for a time and then when I put you out that will be happy too because you have to be snuffed out if you want to come back another day. But let's not think about that now. Now we raise you to the sky and you will be powerful and good and fierce. And you will burn.

12

(ELISE *walks into the therapist's office.* CARRIE *is already there.*)

CARRIE: So how's everything?

ELISE: Good. Good. I'm dating again.

CARRIE: Oh, is he…

ELISE: A police detective investigating my fires.

CARRIE: So you're still…

ELISE: I lit three last night after we made love.

CARRIE: I thought you were stopping.

ELISE: I am stopping. I had to do one more. Well, three more. But that's all. I'm done now. Don't make me feel guilty. I'm trying. But fire is just all I think about.

CARRIE: I don't think it's healthy.

ELISE: I know! Don't look at me like that. I know it's wrong. I'll stop soon.

CARRIE: I think I have to turn you in.

ELISE: What?

CARRIE: I have to.

ELISE: You can't do that.

CARRIE: This can't go on.

ELISE: Well, you better not.

CARRIE: Why not?

ELISE: I'm just saying you better not. Things can catch on fire sometimes I can't control. Like your house. Or your husband. And maybe the firefighters will get bad directions and arrive much much too late to do anything about it and then your house or your husband will be unrecognizable. Things like that can happen. I mean you do what you want, I'm just saying if you like your house and your husband you might want to reconsider your position on whether or not you should mention my firestarting career to anyone. Because I'm really good at eluding cops at least long enough to set everything you love on fire.

CARRIE: I see.

ELISE: Oh, I'm sorry. Did we run over?

CARRIE: It's fine.

ELISE: I didn't mean to take up too much of your time.

CARRIE: It's okay.

ELISE: No, but I feel bad. I don't want to be a difficult client. You can talk more next time. We can even talk about your husband a bit if you want.

13

(LIZ *and* GARY *at a restaurant table.*)

LIZ: I'm sure you know that our drop site was compromised last night.

GARY: What? No, I didn't know.

LIZ: You didn't know that the building in which you hid the documents for me to find burned down last night?

GARY: It did?

LIZ: You didn't know this.

GARY: No, I didn't.

LIZ: We find that hard to believe.

GARY: It's true.

LIZ: It just so happens that you're late getting us some information and then it so happens that when you do drop it off, the place burns down?

GARY: Odd, isn't it?

LIZ: I don't suppose you have a copy of this information we're waiting on.

GARY: No, I don't. But it was really spectacular. You would have loved it.

LIZ: You didn't make a copy?

GARY: No, of course not. It could be traced back to me. Destroy any evidence you said—make no copies.

LIZ: I know what I said.

GARY: It will take a while for me to get information like that again.

LIZ: I don't want excuses. Either give back the money or get us the information. One or the other. But don't make us wait.

GARY: I'll have it again soon. Just give me a couple days.

LIZ: We think you're trying to fuck us over. We don't get fucked over. We do the fucking, if you catch my meaning.

GARY: What do you mean?

LIZ: Never mind what I mean.

GARY: But.

LIZ: You know what I mean.

GARY: But I didn't start the fire.

LIZ: We find that hard to believe.

GARY: I don't even carry matches. I never have. I don't smoke.

LIZ: Get us the information by tomorrow.

GARY: But what if I can prove I didn't start the fire? Can I get an extension?

LIZ: How you gonna do that?

GARY: I don't know. Somehow. I am innocent. Look at my face.

LIZ: I'm putting my neck on the line for you, you understand? They didn't want to hire you.

GARY: I understand.

LIZ: I'll give you a couple days. Bring this so-called arsonist who is not you to us and if we believe you we'll give you an extension. But in the meantime, get that long overdue information to us.

GARY: You got it.

LIZ: You do that. And if I don't see results early next week, I'm going to send someone to come find you. You don't want that.

GARY: You won't have to do that.

Adam Szymkowicz

Liz: Good. I'm glad we understand one a
(louder) It was good to meet you in Austi
see you again this evening.

Gary: Yes, I so enjoyed the orchestra anc
myself with you and your exciting and n
(Exit)

14

(JAKE and ELISE are examining the remains of a fire. JAKE sifts through the ashes with a shovel. TOM, JANE and STU stand nearby in detective garb.)

Tom: Three different fires.

Jane: In three locations.

Stu: Within walking distance.

Elise: What are you doing now?

Jake: Looking for evidence. Just think. While we were in bed last night, someone was out lighting these fires.

Elise: Huh.

Jake: Around that time anyway.

Tom: You think it will last?

Stu: What? Them two?

Jane: There's a pool running back at the station. My bet is on two weeks tops.

Tom: Jake's record? I give 'em a week.

Stu: I think it will work.

Jane: What? You know Jake and women.

Stu: I think it will work.

Jake: And so right now I think the arsonist poured the accelerant, probably acetone, in the window, tossed in what looks like a cigarette and it just went up. I think this one was lit last of the three.

ELISE: How can you tell?

JAKE: Burn patterns. The timing and scope of the fires. I've run some hypotheses.

ELISE: Huh.

TOM: There's no way.

STU: Can't you see he's in love?

TOM: No, I can't.

JANE: I can see that. That's why I think it will last only two weeks. He wants it bad and that will make it worse.

JAKE: The strange thing is…you'll think I'm crazy.

ELISE: What?

JAKE: I think it was a woman.

ELISE: A woman?

STU, JANE, TOM: A woman?

JAKE: I just have this feeling. This feels like female arson.

ELISE: What does that feel like exactly?

JAKE: It's like this fire had some care put into it. Like when a woman makes a bed or folds some clothes or stirs a pot full of vegetables. This fire is like that. Done carefully.

ELISE: Not like a man?

JAKE: My clothes are always in a pile on the floor. I only make my bed if I'm expecting company and even then I don't do it right.

ELISE: I like getting tangled in your sheets.

TOM: She's a spitfire all right.

STU: I wouldn't kick her out of bed for eatin' crackers.

JANE: She wouldn't be in bed. She'd be out all night puttin' out fires.

JAKE: I'm sorry if this is boring.

ELISE: No, not at all.

JAKE: I'm sure you have to get back to the firehouse. I just wanted to see you. To have you near me in the middle of the day while I'm working. I know it's selfish of me.

ELISE: No.

JAKE: To be able to touch you while I'm working.

ELISE: Am I distracting you?

JAKE: No. Perhaps a little. No.

ELISE: I don't want to keep you from your job, Jake.

JAKE: You're not. Say my name again.

ELISE: Jake.

JAKE: Elise.

ELISE: Jake.

JAKE: Elise.

ELISE: Jake.

JANE: Oh, good lord!

JAKE: Is it wrong, to kiss you while I'm working?

ELISE: It might be.

JAKE: I don't care.

(ELISE *and* JAKE *kiss.*)

TOM: Christ.

JAKE: This may be a horrible thing to say but I hope this woman keeps setting fires so I have an excuse to see you as much as humanly possible.

ELISE: That is horrible. I feel the same way. You think it's a woman, huh?

JAKE: I'm almost positive.

ELISE: What do you think the motive is?

JAKE: With a woman you can never tell.

15

(ELISE *and* JAKE *in bed.* ELISE *wears her boots.*)

JAKE: You smell like smoke.

ELISE: I do?

JAKE: In your hair. It stings my eyes.

ELISE: I'm sorry.

JAKE: I like it. It's intoxicating. You're intoxicating.

ELISE: Best be careful then. I know a lot about addiction—been addicted my whole life.

JAKE: Drugs?

ELISE: Fire.

JAKE: I can understand that. My job is less of a job and more of an obsession. I guess firefighting is like that for you too.

ELISE: Yes, that's what I meant. I should go.

JAKE: But you just got here. We just…

ELISE: I know.

JAKE: I wish you would stay.

ELISE: I got things to do. Work. I'm sure you have work too.

JAKE: I should drink coffee and stare at the photos taken at the scene of those last fires and pound my fists on my head and swear I'll catch that arsonist. I should stare and stare at them for that one clue I'm missing and rail at God for only giving me an adequate brain and not making me a staggering genius. I should make models of the fires, map out scenarios, I should smoke one cigarette after another and not sleep and not eat and drink large amounts of Jack Daniels.

ELISE: See, we both have things to do.

JAKE: But I'd rather stay in bed with you and hold you and breathe in the smoke from the nape of your neck.

ELISE: Would your unshaven chin scratch the back of my neck from time to time?

JAKE: It would.

ELISE: Would we fall asleep in each others' arms and then wake at an unusual time to make love again.

JAKE: No doubt about it.

ELISE: I guess I could stay one night. But tomorrow, there is unfinished business I will have to take care of. I will have to make up for time lost here in the bed. But, you're right, let's not think of that now. Let's think of now now.

16

(TOMMY TEN TOES, JIMMY SPLINTERS *and* LIZ *accost* GARY *on the street.* LIZ *is corporate.* TOMMY *and* JIMMY *are a little rougher around the edges.*)

TOMMY: Gary.

JIMMY: Where you goin'?

LIZ: Gary, I'd like you to meet Tommy Ten Toes and Jimmy Splinters.

TOMMY: A pleasure.

JIMMY: How you doin'?

GARY: What's going on?

LIZ: We're very disappointed in you Gary.

GARY: I can drop it off tonight.

TOMMY: Tonight's not so good for us, Gary.

JIMMY: No, it's not.

TOMMY: We kinda wanted it already, see?

LIZ: What do you got?

GARY: Part one.

LIZ: Oh, Gary.

GARY: But I'll find the arsonist and get all the data that I owe you. I just need a little more time.

LIZ: You're making my work much more difficult.

TOMMY: You want I hit him with something heavy?

GARY: What are these guys? They make me uncomfortable.

JIMMY: I'll make you uncomfortable.

LIZ: You see the thing is, my corporation wants to buy your corporation's corporations. You could even get a tip off. You could make some money on the side.

JIMMY: But not unless you play ball.

GARY: I'm working on it.

LIZ: We need you to know we're serious.

GARY: I can see that.

LIZ: We want you to feel it.

(LIZ *nods to* TOMMY *and* JIMMY *who take turns hitting* GARY *in the stomach and face. It hurts. A lot. Then they finish and let him slump to the ground.*)

LIZ: Don't forget about us. Make that drop tonight. Or you won't like our next meeting.

TOMMY: He has soft skin, don't he?

JIMMY: Yeah. It's nice.

17

(Bedroom. Night. JAKE *snores in bed.* ELISE *is partially dressed.)*

ELISE: I could stay. I could stay. Oh, but the light and the heat and the smell, oh the smell. But I could stay. He has smells. He has heat. He has other fine attributes.

The light. The sound of a scraping match. Acetone. Gasoline. Kerosene. The dripping. The pain in the eyes. The light. The heat. The billows of smoke. We have too many buildings, don't you think? Too many construction sites, empty warehouses, all so much fuel. It's a service to take away these extra dangerous buildings. They are in the way, they are dry and cracked and falling down and they need a good match, a good flame a cleansing of the palate, a cleansing of the city.

But I could stay and climb into his arms and breathe his foul comfort of a breath. I could cling to his beliefs in right and wrong and the law. I could give up firestarting right now for good. I could climb back into his bed, dive under the covers. I could warm myself on his broad back, lick the back of his neck, put my small hand around his trigger finger.

But there's the light. There's the heat. There is love and there is love and there are things that I need. And I…

*(*ELISE *folds* JAKE's *shirt, puts it with care on his bed, then kisses him on the forehead.)*

ELISE: Good night.

*(*JAKE *stops snoring.)*

(ELISE exits.)

JAKE: Elise?

18

(CARRIE knits. Enter GARY bloody)

CARRIE: What happened to you?

GARY: They're going to kill me.

CARRIE: What? Who is?

GARY: Don't ask me about my work. I have to go drop something off.

CARRIE: What?

GARY: Don't ask me about my work.

CARRIE: You're bleeding.

GARY: There were three of them.

CARRIE: Let me get a towel. *(Exit)*

GARY: It's not my fault. I know you look at me bleeding and you think it's my fault, but it's not. It's the fault of whoever set that fire. I'm just a bystander who happens to be a white collar criminal. I just got caught up in the mess.

CARRIE: *(Returning with towel)* There now. What were you saying?

(CARRIE cleans GARY up.)

GARY: Nothing. I was just saying it's not my fault.

CARRIE: Of course it isn't.

GARY: I've always been blamed for things I didn't do. Ever since I was a kid.

CARRIE: You've told me this.

GARY: It's true.

CARRIE: I know.

GARY: *(Taking out a suitcase from a hiding place)* I don't even know how to catch an arsonist. Do you set a fire and then wait for them to come? Of course with my luck, they'll see me setting the fire and then there will be no doubt. They will know it was me, which it wasn't of course. Maybe I should do it anyway and then get arrested. They couldn't kill me in jail, could they? I guess they could. *(Takes disk or flashdrive out of suitcase)* I'm not even sure this is something they can use.

CARRIE: What are you talking about?

GARY: Don't ask me—

CARRIE: Because I have a patient who sets fires.

GARY: You do? Why didn't you ever mention it?

CARRIE: I'm not supposed to.

GARY: All this time one of your patients has been setting fires and you never told anyone.

CARRIE: I'm not supposed to talk about my work. Don't ask me about my work.

GARY: But when lives are in danger…like my life.

CARRIE: She threatened me. She said she would burn down the house if I told. And she said she would burn down you too.

GARY: Where can I find her?

19

(At the scene of a fire, ELISE *is barking orders. The fire fighters are running around frantically performing tasks.* GARY *enters and stares at the fire.)*

GARY: Oh shit. *(Exit)*

ELISE: We need more ventilation. Cut off the roof.

TED: I'm on it.

ELISE: Where's that search and rescue team?

SALLY: You think there's someone in there?

ELISE: No, I don't, but just to be on the safe side, better get in there before the building collapses. I want streams of water on the B corner to let the search and rescue in.

BRIAN: You got it.

ELISE: I will put you out. You can burn and burn, but soon you will be smothered. Enjoy your freedom, bring your heat, because in an hour you will be gone.

(Enter JAKE.*)*

JAKE: Hello.

ELISE: What are you doing here?

JAKE: I thought I'd come watch you work. That okay?

ELISE: Of course. I was just surprised is all.

JAKE: You left without saying goodbye.

ELISE: I didn't want to wake you.

JAKE: Where did you go?

ELISE: There was this fire.

JAKE: Aren't you off duty?

ELISE: The fire doesn't know that.

JAKE: But you should let someone else…

ELISE: I can't stay away.

(BRIAN *and* TED *enter carrying* LIZ, *the corporate representative, on a cot. She is badly burned.)*

BRIAN: Look what we found.

LIZ: Unnh.

ELISE: She was inside? What was she doing inside? What were you doing inside?

LIZ: Uunh.

TED: The ambulance is here.

(They carry her off.)

ELISE: You shouldn't have been inside! She shouldn't have been inside. It's an empty warehouse. It's falling down. The homeless around here even stay out of it. What was she doing in there?

JAKE: Relax. It's not your fault. It's the fire's fault.

ELISE: Sure.

JAKE: Any idea what started it?

ELISE: No.

JAKE: Don't worry. We'll get this arsonist, and when we do, we'll make her pay.

20

(LIZ is in hospital bed, badly burned. She moans. Enter TOMMY and JIMMY.)

TOMMY: I can't tell you how sorry we are.

LIZ: Uunh.

JIMMY: We are very sorry.

LIZ: Uunh.

TOMMY: Just tell us what you want us to do.

JIMMY: You want we kill him?

TOMMY: I'll go get him right now.

LIZ: Uunh.

JIMMY: We'll make him pay for what he done to you.

TOMMY: Yeah. We'll kill him.

LIZ: Uunh. Ow.

JIMMY: Does it hurt?

TOMMY: Course it hurts.

JIMMY: Does it hurt a lot?

LIZ: Ow.

TOMMY: Okay, well, we'll go kill him then.

LIZ: No. uunh.

JIMMY: No?

LIZ: I want him to…uunh…feel pain like I feel right now. Is that so much to uunh ask? Can we agree? Ow. He should suffer. He should be in lots of pain for lots of time and should suffer. Uunh. Like I'm suffering. I want you to hurt him uunh. Like no one ever hurt him. Like he's never thought it was possible to be uunh hurt like that. His mind can't conceive uuh of that kind of pain. And his mind will shut down. Ow. And so will his body ahhh until you shock it awake oooh to make it feel more pain. Uuuuuuuunh.

(Pause)

TOMMY: Oh, we can do that, right?

JIMMY: Oh yeah. No sweat. Can we get you anything though? A pillow?

LIZ: Uunh.

21

(At CARRIE's *Office,* CARRIE *and* GARY. GARY *is hiding a tape recorder under the couch.)*

CARRIE: Gary I don't know.

GARY: One of these guys is named Tommy Ten Toes. It's not normal among these people to have ten toes. Imagine what they'll do to me.

CARRIE: We could just tell the cops. Let's do that.

GARY: No, we have to get her to admit to it in your session and then once we have the tape…

CARRIE: Is that legal?

GARY: We're not putting her in jail, we're giving it to these thugs and then I don't have to worry anymore, for a while.

CARRIE: *(Building to hysteria)* No! No! I can't! I can't do it. Don't ask me. I can't do it. Don't ask me. I can't do it! I can't do it!! I can't do it!!!!

(GARY slaps CARRIE.)

CARRIE: No!

(GARY slaps CARRIE.)

CARRIE: I can't!

(GARY slaps CARRIE.)

CARRIE: No!

(GARY is about to slap CARRIE again, but changes his mind.)

GARY: Look at me. Listen. They will kill me. You have to do this. Or else they'll kill me.

CARRIE: They'll kill you?

GARY: Yes. Will you do this for me? Will you save my life?

CARRIE: She'll burn our house down, our whole block down. She'll do it like that. She's not one to be trifled with.

GARY: So we do it carefully.

CARRIE: I'm scared.

GARY: Be brave.

CARRIE: I'm not sure I can be brave.

GARY: You have no choice.

CARRIE: We'll plan it all out?

GARY: I wait outside and once you give the signal I come in.

CARRIE: What's the signal?

GARY: Like a bird call. A cockatoo? A chickadee?

CARRIE: Don't you think it will be weird if I start doing bird calls in the middle of our session? What if I just mention you? I'll just say, "My husband… something"

GARY: I don't know that I'll be able to hear that through the walls.

CARRIE: I'm scared.

GARY: Don't be scared, baby. I'll be right here.

(Enter TOMMY *and* JIMMY.*)*

TOMMY: Gary.

JIMMY: Good to see you.

GARY: Hi guys.

TOMMY: You haven't been to the hospital to visit Liz.

JIMMY: She's hurt awfully bad.

TOMMY: Why haven't you gone to see her?

GARY: I was going to…

TOMMY: It's the guilt, isn't it?

JIMMY: Cuz you tried to burn down a building while she wuz in it.

GARY: That wasn't me.

JIMMY: I've heard that one before.

GARY: Actually, I know who the arsonist is.

TOMMY: Yeah, because it's you.

GARY: No really, I found out who it was.

JIMMY: Oh, so the cops don't know who did it with all their high tech equipment, but you know cuz you're so smart, is that right?

GARY: She told my wife.

TOMMY: "She?"

CARRIE: It's true.

JIMMY: Who are you?

CARRIE: His wife.

GARY: In fact, she'll be here in twenty minutes and I have the room bugged and we're going to get her to admit she did it on tape and then turn her over to you.

TOMMY: Oh you got it all figured out, is that right?

JIMMY: He kind of does.

TOMMY: Well, we'll just wait around and see, then.

GARY: Good. But not here. Not until she's in the office. Then we can wait outside the door.

JIMMY: Well, okay but we're not letting you out of our sight.

GARY: That's fine. If you gentlemen will join me in the hallway.

(The three men exit)

CARRIE: Wait! Hold on. Um…I'm not ready. Hey, I'm not ready!

22

(JAKE *is interrogating a witness, NEAL, on the sidewalk across the street from a fire.*)

NEAL: And then it was on fire all of a sudden. Like it wasn't on fire and then it was. Or I could see no fire and then I could see a fire. And then the whole building went up.

JAKE: And you were just standing there?

NEAL: The whole time. It wasn't me, copper.

JAKE: I didn't ask if it was you.

NEAL: Am I a suspect?

JAKE: Everyone's a suspect. Did you see anyone enter or exit the building?

NEAL: No. No one. I was right across the street the whole time. I like to sit there. It's what I do. Don't judge me. I'll get a job again. Things are rough right now for everyone.

JAKE: And there was nothing out of the ordinary. No one unusual near the fire around that time? Maybe someone carrying a big jug full of flammable liquid and some matches? Maybe a woman?

NEAL: Like I said, there was no one there at all. You don't really suspect me?

JAKE: And when the firemen came, you didn't see anyone hanging around to watch the fire, did you?

NEAL: Some people came and watched, yeah.

JAKE: Anyone you didn't know?

NEAL: No, they were pretty much all from the neighborhood. You know what though? The firewoman there, she showed up really quick.

JAKE: Yeah, she has a gift.

NEAL: She was putting it out right away.

JAKE: She does that.

NEAL: Almost immediately.

JAKE: What do you mean?

NEAL: Before the smoke even.

JAKE: Before the smoke?

NEAL: She's pretty cute, you know, for a fire person. I'd like to see what's inside that rubber raincoat if you know what I mean.

JAKE: Let's change the subject.

NEAL: No, I was just saying I'd like to have sex with her.

JAKE: I'm going to need you to shut up about that.

NEAL: Well, anyway sorry I can't help you. It just went up I guess. What do they call that? Spontaneous combustion.

JAKE: This was no spontaneous combustion. I'd bet my badge on it.

(Pause. JAKE *has a realization.)*

NEAL: What is it?

JAKE: Once when I came out of the shower--the way she was making my bed.

NEAL: Who?

JAKE: Nobody.

NEAL: Well, all right. I don't know then.

JAKE: I'm afraid that I do know, Neal. I'm afraid I know too well how these fires started. It hurts me. It pains me. Right here.

NEAL: Your chest?

JAKE: My heart.

NEAL: Your heart? Why are you looking at me like that? I didn't do it. Don't arrest me.

JAKE: Everything is not about you.

23

(CARRIE *is seated in her office fidgeting.*)

(*Enter* ELISE *carrying a bag.*)

ELISE: I'm sorry I'm late.

CARRIE: Oh, that's okay.

ELISE: Are you all right?

CARRIE: Fine, why do you ask?

ELISE: You're sweating a lot.

CARRIE: I'm fine.

ELISE: You look nervous.

CARRIE: I'm fine. I had a late lunch.

ELISE: What?

CARRIE: Nothing.

ELISE: Listen. Something horrible's happened. There was a woman in the last building I set on fire. I've always been very careful. It's not easy. But no one got seriously hurt on my watch and then some woman dressed like a banker goes into a condemned building I'm burning down. What was she doing there?

CARRIE: So what you're saying is that you burned down the building? The one on the news where the woman was taken out on a stretcher?

ELISE: Are you listening to me?

CARRIE: Isn't that what you said?

ELISE: Of course that's what I said.

CARRIE: I just wanted to be sure that's what you said.

ELISE: What's with you?

CARRIE: Nothings with me. *(Pause)* My husband was just here.

ELISE: Stop talking about your husband.

CARRIE: *(Louder)* I enjoy talking about my husband. I am fascinated by all topics related to my HUSBAND.

ELISE: Can we get back to the session?

CARRIE: Yes, I... What does a cockatoo sound like?

ELISE: I don't think I should come here anymore.

CARRIE: You don't?

ELISE: I don't think you're helping me.

CARRIE: Of course I am. You need me. You really don't think I'm helping you?

ELISE: Well, I'm still setting fires.

CARRIE: But you're in a relationship now. That's going well.

ELISE: Only because I lie to him when he brings up his arson investigations.

CARRIE: Sure, but apart from that, it's going well isn't it? I mean we all have our secrets.

ELISE: But I'm lying to him all the time.

CARRIE: It's not lying. It's keeping secrets which is different. Keeping secrets is okay in a relationship. You wouldn't want me to tell my husband all about your problems would you?

ELISE: That's different.

CARRIE: It is?

ELISE: My life needs to change.

CARRIE: You're finally listening to me.

ELISE: And our sessions need to stop.

CARRIE: KUH KAW!!

ELISE: What are you doing?

CARRIE: I'm the best thing that ever happened to you! KAW KAW! COCK A DOODLE DOO!!

ELISE: Stop that.

CARRIE: Sorry. I'm going to go into the hall for a minute.

ELISE: What's goin' on?

CARRIE: Nothing.

ELISE: The cops are out there, aren't they?

CARRIE: No, not the cops.

ELISE: Who?

CARRIE: I told you to stop setting fires. I warned you. I told you someone would get hurt. This time you burned down the wrong building.

ELISE: You bitch!

(ELISE *slaps* CARRIE.)

CARRIE: Ow. Help!

ELISE: Where are they? In the hallway?

CARRIE: Yes.

ELISE: You can't hear anything in the hallway. Otherwise all your patients would know all the other patients' secrets.

CARRIE: I know, but, HELP!

ELISE: Stop that.

CARRIE: Someone has to stop you.

ELISE: Well, it won't be you. (*She takes a gas can from her bag and starts pouring gas in a line on the floor.*)

CARRIE: My rug! What are you doing?

ELISE: What do you think I'm doing?

CARRIE: This is my office.

ELISE: You're fired.

(ELISE *lights a match and throw it on the ground which goes up in flames**)

(CARRIE *stands there a moment in shock while* ELISE *climbs out the window.*)

(CARRIE *then runs into the hall screaming. A few seconds later* GARY, TOMMY *and* JIMMY *burst into the room followed by* CARRIE. GARY *has an extinguisher and puts out the fire.*)

GARY: Where'd she go?

CARRIE: Down the fire escape.

(*They all look out at the fire escape.*)

24

(*Jake's apartment.* JAKE *is drinking whiskey and smoking. He paces. He puts his face in his hands. Enter* ELISE, *scared.*)

ELISE: Oh, Jake, I'm so glad you're here.

JAKE: What's wrong?

ELISE: They're after me.

JAKE: Who?

ELISE: I don't know. Will you protect me? Will you help me? Will you hide me and hold me and keep me safe?

JAKE: Of course.

ELISE: And not ask any questions?

JAKE: I can't promise that.

ELISE: Let's run away. There's an island in the Mediterranean the tourists don't know about. It never rains there and the hurricanes never hit it and you can pick coconuts and bananas off the trees. You don't need a fishing pole for the fish. There are so many they flop into your arms as if to say *eat me for dinner*. We can go there now. With our pensions we'll live like royalty on the beaches all day swimming with dolphins and at night we'll make love until we become one person.

JAKE: That sounds nice.

(They kiss. JAKE *slaps handcuff on* ELISE.*)*

ELISE: Oh, you're getting kinky.

JAKE: No, you're under arrest.

ELISE: For what?

JAKE: Twelve counts of arson, perhaps more.

ELISE: You're arresting me?

JAKE: It's my job. It's my duty.

ELISE: What about your duty to love?

JAKE: It doesn't mean anything that I love you. Love is meant to be thwarted.

ELISE: That's not true.

JAKE: Anyway, it's not that I don't love you. I just can't afford it right now.

ELISE: That's not true.

JAKE: All this time you've been laughing at me, at my investigating.

ELISE: No, I wasn't. I knew you'd be the one to figure it out. Every time I came to see you I was terrified each time that that time would be the time you would figure it out.

JAKE: I guess that time is now.

ELISE: So what happens now, we go down to the station and you throw the book at me?

JAKE: You'll be tried. I'll get you a good lawyer.

ELISE: I got no chance. I'm guilty. They'll put me away for a long long time.

JAKE: Oh, Elise, things were going so well with us. Why did you have to light fires?

ELISE: Why do you breathe?

JAKE: Yeah.

ELISE: Why do you enforce the law?

JAKE: Right. I just wish...

ELISE: I wish too...I'm sorry. I know it doesn't mean anything, but I am sorry.

JAKE: Me too. Me too.

25

(Three firefighters playing cards, BRIAN, TED *and* SALLY.*)*

BRIAN: Where have all the fires gone?

SALLY: Be thankful.

TED: Sometimes there just aren't any fires for a while and then whoosh a whole bunch.

BRIAN: I wish there was a fire.

(In JAKE'*s apartment,* JAKE *and* ELISE *who is still in cuffs.)*

ELISE: Fire isn't all bad, Jake. There are good things about it.

JAKE: You're wasting your breath. I live and die by the law. She's my quiet mistress who only shows herself when the woman I love turns out to be a deceitful arsonist.

ELISE: I'm sorry.

JAKE: I know.

ELISE: Are we safe here?

JAKE: We're never really safe anywhere. Not any of us.

BRIAN: I can't take it anymore. I need excitement.

(SALLY *grabs* BRIAN'*s face in her hands and kisses him hard.*)

SALLY: How was that?

BRIAN: Yeah. But I mean you're not a fire, are you?

TED: She's a spitfire.

BRIAN: *(To* SALLY*)* Did you look at my cards?

TED: I fold.

ELISE: You gonna put me in jail to get a shiv between the ribs?

JAKE: Why would anyone shiv you?

ELISE: Arsonists aren't popular in the big house.

JAKE: No one's popular in the slammer. Crime ain't a popular pastime.

ELISE: I love you. Don't you see? I've never found anyone like you who I want to be with all the time. I've never been in love before now. It's because I'm a strong woman. Men are intimidated. I thought we had something amazing. Something to cherish. I'm sorry that it turns out once you get to know the real me, the me that wants to burn things, that you can't love me any longer.

JAKE: That's not it.

ELISE: What is it?

JAKE: You lied to me.

ELISE: I had to. Don't you see? But that doesn't mean I didn't love you.

JAKE: I thought I loved a woman once. We went on picnics in Central Park. We took bicycle rides. We

picked out monogrammed towels. We planned to
go away on vacation together on a cruise ship to the
Caribbean. At the last minute they needed me at work.
Crime never sleeps. And so she went alone on a cruise
and met her fiery death. I thought I loved her, but then
I met you and I learned what love really is.

ELISE: Oh Jake.

JAKE: Elise.

(ELISE *and* JAKE *kiss. It becomes passionate and wanton.)*

(The three firefighters have become the three police officers,
TOM, STU *and* JANE. *They clean their guns together.)*

TOM: You ever accept a bribe? Either of you? You can
tell me.

JANE: No, never.

STU: Me either. Well, wait, do sexual favors count?

JANE: You mean you looked the other way in return for
some sex?

TOM: Now, don't judge. Neither of us have to go
through life looking like Stu here does. If that's the
only way the man can get sex…

STU: It was a long time ago.

JANE: I betcha Jake never accepted a bribe.

TOM: Yeah, well not all of us is Jake, are we.

ELISE: Aren't you going to take off the handcuffs?

JAKE: I wasn't planning on it.

ELISE: I have no leverage.

JAKE: I know. I'll take care of everything. Don't worry.

26

(In the street, TOMMY *shoves* GARY. JIMMY *and* CARRIE *follow. The gangsters have hands in their pockets on bulges that imply guns.)*

CARRIE: I mean she's right; I didn't help her stop setting fires. But sometimes it made her so happy I didn't even want to help her. You should have seen the look on her face when she talked about it. It was like when we were first married, Gary how you used to look at me. Why don't you look at me like that anymore? Was it something I did or something I said or did you just grow sick of me or is it something else? Am I a bad person? Is that why you don't look at me like that anymore?

GARY: Carrie—

JIMMY: Hey, now, I think you're great and I bet you're a really good therapist.

TOMMY: Jimmy Splinters is right. I already feel better just being near you. Come on let's get a move on.

*(*TOMMY *shoves* GARY.*)*

CARRIE: I notice you push a lot.

TOMMY: I do?

CARRIE: I don't think you think about other people's feelings much.

TOMMY: Hmmm.

CARRIE: What do you think?

TOMMY: I think I don't think about other people's feelings much.

JIMMY: What's the plan?

TOMMY: We go in there—

JIMMY: Yeah.

TOMMY: And we bring her out.

GARY: Seriously, fellas, you don't really need me for this. I'd just be in the way.

TOMMY: *(Threatening)* I'll give you in the way.

GARY: I work in an office. I'm not used to all this.

CARRIE: But I thought...

GARY: What?

CARRIE: I thought...

GARY: I'm just an ordinary man.

CARRIE: Gary?

JIMMY: Keep moving.

27

(JAKE and ELISE in a post-coital embrace. ELISE is thinking about something.)

JAKE: You want to go start a fire right now, don't you?

ELISE: How did you know?

JAKE: That look in your eye. I always wondered what it meant. Now I know.

ELISE: I have the urge right now hitting me harder than a freight train.

JAKE: Can you resist?

ELISE: I have to, don't I? You got me in cuffs.

JAKE: But if I didn't? A woman as beautiful as you never stays in captivity long. Someone always feels sorry for her and helps her out.

ELISE: I don't put too much stock in the kindness of strangers. I've met too many strangers.

(Pause)

JAKE: I've decided to help you escape.

ELISE: You have?

JAKE: *(Taking her cuffs off)* It goes against everything I believe in, but I can be as stupid as anyone else when the moment presents itself.

ELISE: So, what now?

JAKE: We'll leave together like you said—go live on an island somewhere. Frugally.

ELISE: Can we do that?

JAKE: Shhh. Someone's outside.

ELISE: How do you know?

JAKE: I just know. Take this.

(JAKE *hands* ELISE *a pistol.*)

ELISE: What do I need this for?

(JAKE *turns over a table.*)

JAKE: Quick.

ELISE: What are you doing?

(JAKE *and* ELISE *hide behind the table. As they are disappearing behind it,* TOMMY, JIMMY, CARRIE *and* GARY *enter. They see the two ducking behind the table and immediately* JIMMY *begins shooting. Everyone scatters to hide behind something.* JIMMY *and* TOMMY *begin to shoot at* JAKE. JAKE *is returning fire. Then* ELISE *is too.*)

TOMMY: Give the girl up and we'll let you go.

JAKE: Never.

CARRIE: This is very exciting. Gary, don't you find this exciting?

TOMMY: Get out of the way, coward.

GARY: I'm not a coward.

JAKE: Whoever you are you are breaking and entering. I am a man of the law.

JIMMY: Don't lay your bad trip on me, copper.

JAKE: I can have the place surrounded. *(To himself)* If I could just get to my phone. *(To* TOMMY *and* JIMMY*)* You're in big trouble gentlemen. I suggest you go right now because if you don't, either you're leaving in cuffs or you're leaving dead.

TOMMY: I can stay here all day. I'm not afraid of a few flying bullets.

JIMMY: Me either. Jimmy Splinters has never been the first one to leave during a shootout.

TOMMY: It's a matter of pride for him.

JAKE: The only time I leave a fight before it's over is the time they take me out in a body bag.

TOMMY: That time may be today.

ELISE: Will you boys stop posturing please?

CARRIE: Let them posture. I like posturing.

(Shooting resumes. TOMMY *gets shot and falls.)*

TOMMY: I been hit.

JIMMY: Tommy!

GARY: Is he okay?

TOMMY: Tell my mother I love her.

JIMMY: I will.

*(*TOMMY *dies.* GARY *picks up his gun.)*

JIMMY: His mother's gonna be real upset.

JAKE: I'm real upset at his mother.

JIMMY: I'll make you pay, copper.

GARY: Yeah, copper. We both will.

*(*GARY *shoots at* JAKE.*)*

CARRIE: What are you doing?

GARY: I've always pretended like I was some kind of action hero. I started trading secrets just to not have a boring life. I wanted to be like some kind of agent, like in the movies. But the truth is, this is the first time I've ever held a gun.

CARRIE: How does it feel?

GARY: It feels good.

CARRIE: You don't have to prove anything to me.

GARY: I'm proving something to myself.

CARRIE: Oh, okay then.

(Everyone except CARRIE is shooting. There is probably rolling and ducking and shouting.)

(JIMMY gets shot and falls.)

JIMMY: Ahhhh.

GARY: Jimmy Splinters.

JIMMY: I'm done for. Find the way to go on without me.

GARY: I never really got to know you, Jimmy Splinters.

JIMMY: Blame it on the man. Ain't no cop never understood no street justice. *(He dies.)*

GARY: *(As he's shooting)* You bastards!!

JAKE: We need to make a run for it.

ELISE: Kiss me first.

(ELISE and JAKE have a long kiss under cover while GARY shoots at them. Then they finish the kiss and both start shooting back as they run to the door.)

(GARY gets shot and falls. CARRIE rushes to his side.)

GARY: Unh. They got me.

CARRIE: Oh, Gary. You were brave.

GARY: Was I? All I ever wanted was to be brave. And someone special.

CARRIE: You are special.

GARY: So are you.

(JAKE *and* ELISE *escape.*)

CARRIE: Stay with me.

GARY: I can't.

CARRIE: You're dying.

GARY: Yes. I'm another pawn. Look at them all. All of them pawns. No one dies for countries anymore. We die for corporations. *(He dies.)*

CARRIE: Noooooo!

28

(At the docks. Sound of a foghorn. Boats, seagulls. JAKE *and* ELISE *are looking at a boat.)*

ELISE: We can start our life together now.

JAKE: I'm going to put you on this boat, but I need to know—

ELISE: It wasn't me.

JAKE: What?

ELISE: It wasn't me set the fire that killed your girlfriend.

JAKE: Oh, that. I know that. What I need to know—

ELISE: What?

JAKE: I need to know...

ELISE: Yes?

JAKE: I need to know you won't burn this boat down. Promise me you won't set fire to the boat.

ELISE: Of course I won't.

JAKE: I just couldn't handle it.

ELISE: You're coming with me though. You have to come with me. I'm a strong independent woman capable of starting a new life by herself, but that doesn't mean I don't want you to come with me.

JAKE: Oh, Elise. I can't come with you. My blood is the blood of a detective. I wouldn't be able to stop myself from hauling you off to jail. I can hold it at bay while you get on this boat. I can let it leave without trying to find out where the boat is going, but that's your only hope. And it's not that I don't love you because I do, but I don't know how long I can keep you from myself. So I need to know you'll not perish in a flaming boat. I need to know you won't burn yourself up. You have to convince me because otherwise I'm taking you to the station right now. Say it.

ELISE: I won't set the boat on fire.

JAKE: Tell me you'll never light a fire again.

ELISE: I…

JAKE: You don't have to mean it. You just have to make me believe it.

ELISE: Oh, Jake.

JAKE: Elise. Say it.

ELISE: I'll never again touch anything incendiary. I've learned my lesson about playing with fire. Not so much as a cigarette or a lifesaver between my teeth in the dark.

JAKE: Thank you.

ELISE: You'll come find me someday? You'll stop living the life of the law and come look for me?

JAKE: It's always possible.

ELISE: Is it?

JAKE: I could retire for good and change myself into the kind of person who has no care about right and wrong.

ELISE: I'd like that.

(Foghorn)

JAKE: That's your boat. You should go.

ELISE: Kiss me.

JAKE: One last time.

(ELISE and JAKE kiss. Then, the sound of a gunshot. Enter CARRIE pointing a gun at them.)

CARRIE: I want justice.

JAKE: Justice?

CARRIE: For the death of my husband.

JAKE: No one ever found justice in the chamber of a forty-five.

CARRIE: I demand justice. You killed my husband.

JAKE: He was shooting at us.

CARRIE: He'd be alive right now if you weren't a pyromaniac.

ELISE: You're my therapist. Maybe you could have been more convincing.

CARRIE: I tried. Can't you see I tried?

JAKE: Put the gun down.

CARRIE: I just wanted to be good at something!

JAKE: You're hysterical. Lower your gun.

CARRIE: No. Someone has to pay. People can't just do whatever they want and get away with it without regard to how it affects other people. I won't stand for it anymore. You're a house burner and a killer and you took my husband--you took him--you took him-you—

(CARRIE *shoots but* JAKE *steps forward and takes the bullet himself.*)

(CARRIE *drops the gun, shocked at what she's done. And* JAKE *falls into* CARRIE *but manages to handcuff her to himself.*)

ELISE: Jake!

(*Foghorn*)

JAKE: Get on that boat and don't let me know where it's going.

ELISE: But—

JAKE: Go! Go! And don't look back. Forget me. No, remember me. No, forget me.

(ELISE *exits to the boat.*)

CARRIE: Singapore.

JAKE: What?

CARRIE: The boat's going to Singapore.

JAKE: I'm sorry. I didn't hear you.

CARRIE: You should listen more.

JAKE: You're going away for a long time. (*Makes phone call*) I'm going to need an ambulance and a patrol car. I'm at the seaport. Make it quick.

CARRIE: So this is my life. It's not what I imagined. Jail. Maybe it will be a nice change of pace.

JAKE: Did you see that?

CARRIE: What?

JAKE: It looked like an open flame on the deck of that boat. Well, it's gone now. And so is she.

END OF PLAY

CPSIA information can be obtained
at www.ICGtesting.com
Printed in the USA
BVHW041925260520
580362BV00015B/404